My Hands
Have Vertigo

Jennifer Finley

Likesgoodbooks Press

Ronan, Montana

Likesgoodbooks.com

likesgoodbooks

ISBN: 0692832246
ISBN-13: 978-0692832240

DEDICATION

I dedicate this book to you, for you have always been worth loving.

Contents

ACKNOWLEDGMENTS

Versions of the poems "A Woman's Love," "Holy Land," and "Step into the Light," appear in the play *Belief.*

"My Hands Have Vertigo" was published in *Grantmakers in the Arts Reader.* Volume 25, No. 2, Summer 2014.

"Deer," "Magpies," and "What My Cat Would Say to Me," were published in *Dark Matter*, October 2016, Issue #4.

"Hawaiian and Salish," and "My Wild Horse of a Heart," were published in *Poems Across the Big Sky* volume II 2016.

I'm so deeply grateful for the kindness and love of my friends. Thank you for believing in me Lynette Christensen, Sydney Seyfert, Julie Cajune, Jenifer Blumberg, David J. Spear, Mark Gibbons, Robbie Liben, Marcile Echeverry, and Virginia L'Bassi. Thank you Beth Costigan for beautiful cover photo you provided and Alexa Greene for the photo you took of me.

FORWARD

Like the Monarch butterfly, Jennifer Finley has emerged once again in this collection stronger and more beautiful than in her previous poetic lives, *What I Keep* and *What Lasts*, both award-winning books back when she was known as Jennifer Greene. And just as that third transformation of the Monarch blossoms into a super butterfly, Finley's *My Hands Have Vertigo* reveals a woman liberated from the limitations of a failed relationship.

A poet of Salish heritage born and raised on the Flathead Reservation in Montana who came of age in New Mexico and Arizona where she fell in love, married, and birthed three children, Finley refined her poetic voice with the help of the gifted poet/teacher, Jim Simmerman, at Northern Arizona University.

Jennifer believes . . . *loving is / the bravest thing we will ever do.* And since this collection was written after divorce, she has considered the topic deeply. *I do not have the heart of a gambler / placing wild bets like I have nothing to lose.* She understands the risks all too well, but she will not deny her desire for love, that *wild horse of a heart* that needs to feel the connection to all things— including men. She has learned to tread their unknown space: *Why does talking to you feel like I'm swimming in deep ocean water / where my bare feet touch nothing? I cannot fathom your depth.*

The first section of this book is filled more with longing and desire than sorrow or loss, as if she has given her wild horse of a heart the chance to gallop and dance after so many years of cloistered restraint, even the long lines of the poems in this section run on with the exuberant rhythm of hooves pounding an open landscape. She honors her dear *"beautiful heart" / for it is you who has always loved me.*

The second section, *Farewell*, is comprised of poems to family and friends. It is full of sea imagery and directed at her ex-husband who introduced her to the ocean. In its open exploration of divorce, this thoughtful reasoning of the head and the heart seems an attempt to explain herself—and first and foremost, she is *not okay*. Some of these confessions are painful, some are angry, and some are forgiving.

This wonderfully heartbreaking and sorrowful journey is a rebirth and a celebration. Life is full of regrets and losses, but the world is turning now, life is blooming and dying all around us, our children are growing older, and that's where Jennifer's poems take us, into our own dizzy vertigo, the joy of the spin, knowing that what matters most is honoring one's heart and being true to the spirit, the magic of love.

Mark Gibbons, poet

Missoula, Montana

Chapter 1 MY HANDS HAVE VERTIGO

A Woman's Love

I am love. I am a woman's love.
My tears have born children into this world.
I don't care what you look like.
I don't care what degrees you have or don't have.
I don't care how broken you feel.
I love you because I am a woman's love,
and I love every sliver of you.
I sing you love songs without words.

You never said you were sorry for anything,
but I forgive you.
No matter how many times you broke my heart,
I still believe in you.
No matter how many times I was crushed with disappointment,
I still believe in magic because I am a woman's love.
I want you to swim across raging rivers for my hand.
When the world is chaos and in a state of disaster,
I want you to piece together all that is strong inside you,
and call my name.
I want you to do the courageous thing and reach for me
because loving is the bravest thing any human can do.

The rivers give my arms strength.
The moon weaves its beauty into my hair like spider webs.
These mountains kiss my dreams with magic.
Deer, geese, and bears bless me with songs.
The wind breathes holy medicine into body when I run.
This land has courage because it loves me.
This land has been faithful to me
even when I have not been faithful to myself.

We must remember what loves us,
and we must be brave enough
to reach for love, no matter how long it's been.
It's never too late to love or be loved.

If you believe that love will find you, then love will find you.
Love will float through your open windows
when your eyes are closed. If you want love to find you,
uncurl your fists and reach for rivers.
Let the currents wash away any voice that
says you are not worthy of moonlit songs.

Let's forget where we've been.

Let our hands be reckless.
Let our mouths taste what is sweet.
Let our feet stumble into trouble.
Let's let love wash us clean like summer starlight.
Tonight, let us all sing without words
and let us love because loving is
the bravest thing we will ever do.

My Heart is Mysterious

I wish I could stop wondering
what your mouth would feel like
pressed against me.

Sometimes, I want to fill your hands
with my body.

I keep wanting to spill words on paper
and send them to you
because I know your eyes
will touch the shape of each letter.

There are men who would have me,
but my heart is mysterious
with her own secret longings.
Even I don't know why
she picked you.

When you were a little boy,
did you ever roll down grassy hills in short sleeved shirts?

As a man, what do you do
to have some good, delicate pleasure against your bare skin?

I know you are afraid I will break you,
but if you wanted me
I'm afraid
love would break us both open
because that's what it does
the same way fire opens pinecones
or the same way rivers carve through stone.

You and I would never be the same,
either together or apart.

My Hands Have Vertigo

My heart loses her equilibrium
when I hear your voice.
My words taste drunk,
and I forget
what I'm not supposed to say.
I say things like I'm attracted to you,
and you are so appealing to me.

Sometimes, my hands have vertigo.
My palms are dizzy with longing.

You say you measure my words carefully,
and contemplate everything I say.

As you gather my thoughts like fireflies
that land on your bare arms,
what will you do with them?

I'm No Gambler

You are the most cautious and mysterious man I have ever met.
Somehow, this has prompted me to be reckless with words.
There is part of me that knows better,
but I'm tired of trying to be good.
I gambled and rolled bold words across state lines for you.
My brazen admiration wasn't enough
to make you lick the palm of my hand.
I was wrong about many things.

I do not have the heart of a gambler
placing wild bets like I have nothing to lose.

We Danced

for Diego

Music dances in your words like fat rain from luscious skies.
Your strong hands have watched me and spun me backwards.
Your fingers carve sentences in English and Spanish.
You brush pictures of lovers and a broken heart onto empty pages.

When your hands gaze at me, I feel exposed.
Your eyes ask me questions that catch me off guard
and pieces of me scatter like a flock of blackbirds broken loose
from blizzard winds, and my face gets warm.

I've danced close enough to you to smell your mouth
and feel the hardness of your chest against the softness of mine.

Why does talking to you feel like I'm swimming in deep ocean water
where my bare feet touch nothing? I cannot fathom your depth.

Springtime

In this last bit of winter
with spots of ice and hardened snow
spilled across Missoula sidewalks,
you reached across the darkness and held my hand.

You kissed me
like a little bird drinking water.

Tracing the contours of your face
with the tips of my fingers
reminded me of springtime
when the earth feels messy and passionate
with shooting star purple
buttercup yellow
and stem green thrown everywhere.

Your Adam's apple tasted
like hard fruit eager to ripen.

When you breathed my name
you swept me in a direction
I had not planned on going.

I felt the wild, deep pull of you
like salty ocean tides.

Thank you for such beauty
strong and fleeting as spring
which never returns the same way twice.

You Asked

You asked me why I like you & what I see in you.

Part of it is how animal luminous your eyes are in the dark &
the way moonlight curves around your bare neck and shoulders.

Then there is the way red wine tastes on your breath &
how my stomach swims when you kiss me.

Your long, thin fingers penetrate
my day dreams when I sit quietly
and look out the window at still magpies.

When you sleep, you look as content as clouds
stretched above an ocean at night.

I like the way I feel when you look directly at me &
how you never avert your gaze from mine.

Part of my attraction to you is as mysterious
as anything else that is magic and new to this world
like the beginning of a song hummed beneath the sky for the first time.

Lost Causes

At one time or another, we have all been a lost cause.
Maybe it was the time we fell in love with someone we knew was wrong
who didn't fit in with our friends or anything we thought we wanted,
yet we hurled ourselves into that union like a kamikaze who hopes to be the exception
who prays at the last minute to crawl from the guaranteed wreckage unharmed.

Maybe it was at a moment when all hope drained away
like a leaf that's lost all its green color and all it can do is fall
to make room for some other leaf to take its place.

Maybe it was an evening when we felt smashed with disappointment
and thought that being loved back was only for other people, not us.

I suspect you already think you don't deserve me
like you are some sort of lost cause because you've made mistakes, but
you are beautiful and good.
Your golden light is all I feel spreading across my bare chest
when you wrap your long fingers in my dark hair.

You left before I could tell you I, too, know how it is
when one's own goodness seems like some sort of mirage
that feels like too much to hope for.

It is never easy for me to trust a man's hands or a man's assurances.
You left before I could tell you, despite my own past, I believe in magic, and God, and miracles.

Some suicide missions fail because we are meant to live.
Maybe new sprouts on a branch love the vibrancy of orange and yellow on the ground.
Maybe fallen leaves look up and find comfort and hope in anything brave enough to be born.

There is a reason you and I reached for each other.
Perhaps we are not as lost as we thought.

I Drove

for DM

Once, I drove back in time to see you.
down a two lane Montana highway
past once opulent hotels, man heavy bars
packed with empty cars parked outside.

As I drove, the only stations I could get
were hits from the 80's and some religious music.
I bought coffee in Havre and rolled down the window.
I ran over one rabbit and one gopher.
You were waiting for me in your bed,
and you left the door open.

I Would Have

for DM

Your love was like a swarm of angry red roses
against my mouth that left me swollen, aching.

Your smell breathed itself inside me when you walked into a room,
and I could taste you without kissing you.

Each morning before the sun came up, you kissed me before work.
You asked me to read my poems to you at your kitchen table.

I would have stayed with you forever if you asked me one more time.

My Stay

for DM

I watched you get dressed in the darkness, wordlessly
your shirt slipped over your bare back and stomach.
Somehow the smell of coffee seeping into the lightless room
and the sound of your work boots walking on the kitchen floor
felt more intimate than the taste of your mouth from the night before.
I liked the way you swiftly brushed your hair after you showered
and the way your skin smelled like both open sky and rolling prairie.

It feels odd knowing that I'll never see you again. I'll never bump into you
at the grocery store, and I'll never see you accidentally at the movie theater.
This oppressive humid sadness feels like a summer heat wave
that prevents me from sleeping. Eventually, I'll stop melting
into tears when I'm alone, and I will yearn for the crisp open of autumn
when the world is orange and yellow, and I can inhabit a season
that has no memories of you inside it.

Metal Worker

for Kevin

The veins in your forearms are thick as hard boot laces,
and your hands are scratchy as a cat's lick on my skin.
Your hands build bridges and melt pieces of metal together.

People drive across bridges you built and put their weight
on benches you made not knowing the man who touched
the things they depend upon to keep them safe.

Some nights, your fingers move across my body with the focus
& slow precision of a man spinning a combination lock twisting
me one way & then another until I open deep parts of myself to you.

We walked hand in hand in old mining towns like Butte & Anaconda
where men once sank deep into the earth's darkness and smell
to bring unmelted metal and unpolished gems to the earth's light.

You walked beside me on sidewalks stamped with the names of dead men while
thin snowflakes curved around us in the dark. We kissed in front of empty houses
that once held people who made love to each other when they were alive.

You and I stood outside beneath stars that were there before we cried our first breath
into the world. So many beautiful things in this world will melt like snow.
Until then, curve your hand around mine, and let me savor the taste of your mouth.

Filled

Sometimes I'm a blue clay bowl
filled with an old longing

to reach out and cup your hands,
but I'm empty from giving

and never getting anything in return.

Still No Word From You

There are sharp moments when sorrow hits me
like bursts of unexpected sheets of rain
blowing me sideways, soaking my brown skin.

My own tears are lost on my silent face.
All I can taste is salt.
My arms lose their buoyancy.

Deafening waves of rejection and non-responsiveness
from you crash against me.

My heart will remain beautiful and strong
no matter what you do not say to me.

But I am ravaged and tattered like wet paper.

I Have No Reason

I have no reason to believe in love, except that I have loved.
I loved stupidly, honestly, drunkenly, carelessly.
Love has a mind of its own.
I have loved many times and didn't know why
some of the men I loved didn't love me back.

For you, I pray this.
If you love someone who does not love you,
may your hands protect the softness of your own throat
and give your voice mercy.
May you press both your hands against your chest to stop yourself
from arguing with something as drunk & wild as love.

Thank You

moonlight that shines upon my dark hair
ocean waters for making me feel both humble and strong
dear beautiful heart for it is you who has always loved me

Butterflies

My throat felt like a clouded sky
as I stood in the 400-year-old building
made with stones. Someone's hands
carved stars into the ceiling.
Naked men once took baths in that building.
Later, men prayed to divine parts of themselves.
After that, the domed structure curved
around paintings as an art museum
that captured daydreams.
My lips tasted like night fog.
My hands flickered like stars.
I felt like the woman in a painting
who had orange butterflies for hair.

A Woman

I am a Salish woman.
I am a spiritual woman.
I am a Cree woman.
I am a good woman.
I am a Chippewa woman.
I am a strong woman.
I am a brown woman.
I am a beautiful woman.

Holy Land

Tonight, I'm going to swim slow in a Montana river alone,
and I will not wash away into nothing. Swarms of black minnows
will swim around my brown legs. My hair will smell like river.
No matter what, I am this holy land
where generations of Salish medicine women have sung prayers into the rocks.

White birds and soft green leaves fly into my tears with good medicine.
These mountains dance strength into my feet with every touch.
My face is the face of this land.
Some days my hair flies like a flock of blackbirds in the wind.
Some days I am a blizzard of sorrow, and my heart shines like snow.
Some days I am the beauty of a turtle's shell rising from the surface of a still pond.
Other days I am the voice of wisdom in a lightning storm.
Sometimes I am waterfall mist with a thousand hands that love your face.

I am this holy land where generations of love songs rain like feathers from the sky.
I am this holy land where my great-grandchildren's names
will be loved by the rivers, prayed for by old women, and remembered by every stone.

December in Missoula

Today, it's maybe two degrees in Missoula.
This bitter cold makes the skin on my face tight.

In a café with a wall made of mostly window,
I drink black coffee that tastes like a flower in my mouth.

I remember being in Hawaii where a man gave me a lei
strung with orange flowers that were edible.

His mother taught him how to make leis
and once scolded him for eating the earthy petals.

The day I met that man, I walked across a pancake restaurant
with my skirt tucked into my underwear.

In the coffee shop here in Missoula, there's a man in shorts at the next table
and a white guy outside with no gloves on his tattooed fingers lights a cigarette.

This cold makes my shoulders hurt from shivering & I long to stand
on warm ground where frost has never crawled up the windows like ivy.

My ancestors were born of this land, and my brown skin is made for it,
yet when I'm in a place where the sun ripens across the sky every day, part of me wakes up.

Sometimes, in this cold place, I feel constricted, my fists closed in my pockets
when I deeply want to reach open-handed into soft dirt and smell earth.

I must remind myself that seeing my breath in my car is part of life here,
and even the coldest times, when leaves are dormant, there is beauty in this winter silence.

Hawaiian and Salish

for my beautiful Hawaiian friends

Hawaiian

You are made of orange flowers,
and the smell of salt water.

You are made of songs filled with mist
and hands that know how to dance.

You are made of rainbows
and rain that beats with a faithful heart.

You are made of land that's fit for the kings,
warriors, and queens you have always been and will always be.

You are made of ocean magic and stars
that will always sing you the way home.

You are made of lava from the core of all that is
and all that has the courage to reach the sun's love.

Salish

We are made of long, dark winters
and cold times that taught us how to weave stories and pray.

We are made of deer leaping through snow
and mountain lions quietly breathing and walking in the woods.

Our hands are made of purple mountain flowers
and earth medicine that will never leave us.

We are made of the smell of fresh water,
pine needles, and handfuls of wet river stones.

We are made of coyote story mischief
and animals that come to us when we need them.

We are made of magic dreams and love songs
that flicker in our hair like butterflies landing on wet leaves.

Together

Together, we are beautiful and strong.
The same stars watch over and guide both of us.

How could we doubt our beauty
when we look at our mountains or swim in our waters?

How could we doubt our strength
when snow and ocean tides are stronger than anyone who doesn't love us?

When we hear wind sing through our trees
how could we forget how much we are meant to be here?

We are these waters. We are these lands. We are still here. We are together.
We are connected by the stars. We are connected by love.

Rez Man

for Derek

One night you came to my house and changed my tire
late in the evening after it rained all day, and the ground was cold and wet.

You are the first non-relative I trusted to babysit my kids.
You can make Greek sauces, and you know how to cook salmon.

You are strong, over six feet tall. Your hands can crush another man's pride,
but you are not a man who puts fear into anybody smaller than you.

I am your mother's friend. Do you know how deeply she wishes for everything good for you?
Your mother would forsake you for nothing in this world & for that you are wildly blessed.

You are Salish like me, and we are both loved by this land,
yet, for different reasons, we know how hard it is to live here.

It still surprises me when men are kind & don't give me reasons to be afraid.
Thank you for your kindness, for it gives me hope in this place.

Clay

Before you had a man's voice and a man's thoughts,
I knew you when I was the little girl who lived down the road.
Back then, I frequently got lost staring out some window
daydreaming or praying for a catastrophic flood
that would carry me away or at least cancel school.

Your mother was my dad's second grade teacher.
She knew him when he had little hands.

After 20 years of not seeing you, one August evening
you walked into a coffee shop and recognized me.
I tried to picture the boy who used to sit next to me on the bus,
and my mind could not swim back to that place,
yet you were as familiar to me as Twin Lakes or Valley Creek
or some other part of Arlee I've always known.

Later, in your yard, you stopped beneath the branches
of an apple heavy tree. You reached toward the sky
with an open hand, and I loved how you talked and reached
so casually toward something ripened, beautiful and red.

So many things in this life fade too quickly
like autumn leaves covered by early snow,
the sound of a hummingbird's wings that fly away too quickly,
or the taste of a kiss you want to remember.

Inside the house you grew up in, you offered me chocolate cake.
Your mother sat at the table and looked at you
the way I look at my children when I remember
how grateful I am for the way they've grown into my life,
and how we sustain each other like forest and animal.

Montana Boy

for Don

Grew up in Wolf Point
the only white guy on the basketball team.

When he was a boy, nobody went to school
after the first snow blanketed the ground
because they were out tracking deer.

At 10, he bought his first
horse from an Indian man.

Son of a mother who loved books.
Son of a mother who said he wasn't better
than anybody else no matter their skin color.

Said he was a hard son to raise,
but, out of respect for his mother,
he still attends church every week
to hear another man talk about God.

After being a soldier in Vietnam,
he returned to Stockman's Bar in Missoula
altered by war in ways most men never speak of,
and the bar tender remembered his name
and acted as if only an ordinary weekend had passed.

Though some memories are tangled as a knot of baling twine,
or as painful as falling against barbed wire,
or sweet as wind in the rolling hills of eastern Montana,
there are men who have hearts strong enough to still be kind.

Lilac

In the winter, I dream powerful earth prayers.
On the tip of one branch I hold the memories of a thousand years of days.
In the deepest bitter cold and winter darkness, I live my life.
I survive until spring and open my purple hands to butterflies and bird wings.
People can smell my love songs in the spring.
Then my hands wither come summer, and I get ready for my long sleep
because I have important dreams to dream.
Long, dark times taught me how to pray,
how to gather my strength, how to savor every touch of your hand.

Bitterroot Day

It rained gentle, sloppy, splashy, mud puddly rain.
I went to the Bitterroot mountains alone
whispering random melodies and prayers.
In this month, the end of the hunting month,
the last of our people moved away in 1891.

In my ancestral home that still belongs to my heart,
I stopped at a second-hand store called Little Bit of Hope,
but I did not buy any sweat-stained shoes worn by someone else.
The people who now live where my ancestors lived make me feel uneasy.
I do not trust them to be good stewards of this land.

My blood memory is strong and knows the pitch of the land's voice.
The lands knows the smell of my hair. This land knows
my daughter and both my sons by name.
Once, women who looked like me
woke up on fall mornings and heard river water, rain
and their own children playing, and breathing all over our land.
My ancestors prayed for their children,
and I will always pray for mine.

Child

for Alexa, James, and Johnny

I would give up my language for you.
I would learn new words for turtle, shoelace, and wet snow.
For you, I would give up my country, my homeland.

As you lie in bed under soft blankets,
do you know how much you matter to me?
I have not been so lucky in matters of love.

I was born into a blizzard of sadness
that, at times, I've struggled to crawl away from
with blood on my hands and my mouth.

There are strings of days where it takes all my breath
to stand, but each morning before I rise to face what I must face,
I pray for each of you by name.

May each of you know how beautiful you are
even if nobody is there to tell you so.

May each of you know how precious you are
even in moments of rejection and disappointment.

I am sorry, but my love will not be enough
to protect you from those who may not love you back.

Child, know this.
Love is magic.
It can rise from nothing.
I am humble and small,
but I can give you something
as fine and noble as love.

School Concert

Tonight, in a middle school gym my daughter sings with other people's children.
These children's faces are unlined by maturity or the sun's heat.
The gym has artificial, harsh light, and everybody's lips look purple.

As I shift on the hard bleacher and listen,
I think about how at this very moment,
there is a war going on.
Men with sweaty hands are holding guns.

In this place filled with children's music,
even the toilets are filled with clean water.
All these girls are well fed.
Nobody in this room fears a sniper's bullet hollowing any part of the boys here.

We are surrounded by luxury.
How many children are there right now who want to sing with other children but can't?
This night, how many children will fall asleep with gunshots dancing across their dreams?
This night, how many mothers would give anything to hear their child's voice one more time?

What if There Were No Such Thing as a Fairy Tale?

What happens to little girls who grow up
and never get saved from washing socks and plates?
What happens to little girls who become women who slave away
for one crumb of approval from a thankless man?

What happens when ugly sisters become teachers, bartenders or mothers
who live to tear a beautiful woman to shreds and laugh at her clothes?
What happens when ugly sisters tell a busy woman she isn't doing enough?

What happens to the little boys who will never be princes
or charming or kind to a woman who needs protection?
What happens to a man when he takes a woman's money
and spends all her youth?

What would happen if more women plunged into summer lakes,
sang their own names to the night sky and at least one solid mountain?
What would happen if more women wore their most beautiful dresses,
threw crumbs on the floor, and swept their hair back?
What would happen if more women felt like red jewels?
What would happen if more of us felt as beautiful as rain falling on rivers?

40

I sit alone the night before I turn 40.
Divorced. Disowned.
I will receive no gifts this year.

I have no money to buy myself anything
or take myself anywhere special.
Nobody is asking me to dance.

Lung sore and fever weak with a chest cold,
I sit in bed reading Irish poetry.
I listen to French music that feels like red lipstick on my mouth.

I no longer mind dancing alone or singing badly.
Any fucking day, I would rather turn 40 alone
than rip open another gift from someone else who never deserved me.

Somewhere

Somewhere, there is a man who has stood in bare feet beneath the stars,
and he has hummed songs about love I haven't heard yet.

Somewhere, there is a man who doesn't want to be a boy.

Somewhere, beneath this pulsating sky, he is breathing.
I don't know if he is asleep or awake or what his face smells like.
His hands are waiting to reach for me and only me.
Someday, he will write my name on paper.

Lost

This morning I tried to walk outside
but a freezing fog enveloped each exposed pebble in a clear layer of ice.
Every surface was slippery, and I could only wobble tiny steps without falling.

A friend once broke her wrist in such weather when she tried to break a fall.
She's the one who told me to take small steps when everything is ice.

In years and miles, I'm so far away from who I thought I'd be.
I've always had a poor sense of direction.
Too easily lost.
Somehow I have always managed to find my way in foreign cities
where the only words I knew were hello and thank you.
I've been lost in so many parking lots unable to find my own car.
When I'm lost, part of me always wants to give up or cry,
yet there is always some force that pushes me down one more unknown street,
and then another until I see something I recognize.

I just got divorced, and there are terrains and textures of new men and new conversations
that feel utterly foreign to me, and I am completely disoriented.

I'm overwhelmed, and I just want to sleep in a bed where I can smell the ocean.
Everything feels slippery and murky, and I want to move faster,
but I am afraid to fall for the wrong man again.
For now, I don't know the way,
and I'll have to take little steps until the fog clears.

What My Cat Would Say to Me

Sometimes I like to stretch out belly to dirt my face close to the earth.
I can hear things you can't understand. I would like to tell you
how much I love your hands on my head, my back, my ribs.
I would like to tell you what it's like to climb a pine tree at night beneath the stars
and how all living creatures have wise things to say.

There are times when all I can do is sit next to your arms
when you weep silently in the wee hours of the night.
I wish I could tell you how much the trees love you,
how much the moon loves you, and how there is good magic in your dreams.

Tonight, when you sleep, I will look at your closed eyes in the moonlight.
I will listen to you breathing, and I will purr a thousand lullabies just for you.

Deer

At night, I lie beneath the stars, year round.
I smell like open sky, snow, and lake water.
Nobody has to tell me my face is holy and beautiful.

I dream in a language your people used to know.
Woman, I see you and your children looking at me
through car windows and house windows.
I smell your children's breath when they step outside.
The blood in your veins is not so different than mine
that pulses warm on moonlit winter nights
as you listen to your offspring breathing.

We are not so different. We both gave birth.
We both smelled danger in a man's angry voice.
We both know when to run and when to hide.
We both know how to kick with our strong legs.
We both know we are the ones on which someone else depends.

We are the ones with the power of moonlight in our hair.
We are the ones with the beauty of this land imbedded in us.

Seagulls

It's too bad seagulls can't look into each other's eyes,
smell the salt on each other's faces, and sing out to the moon's pull
instead of fighting over nothing
when something as beautiful as the ocean
is calling, calling, waiting for them.

Magpies

My dad used to say magpies were a nuisance bird.
I seem to see them everywhere I go.
Magpie flocks flutter in the pine trees in my yard.
They eat dog food from my dog's dented metal dish.

I know what it's like to feel unwanted, like my existence,
my words are a nuisance and are not welcomed.
I will never kill a magpie.
I will remember magpie mothers
who must feed their young no matter what.
I will remember black hooded heads and black eyes
that know these trees and lakes and deer from the sky.
I will remember that nobody can be wanted all the time.

One time or another, we have all been magpies.

Still

I still wonder if I would have been brave enough
to let you slide your hand up my skirt
if you had been brave enough to try it.

I wanted you to.
You looked at my brown bare legs but never touched me.

I was so young then.
I was afraid of my own brambled wildness.

I was an overgrown jungle temple where
wild prayers blossomed like pink flowers in my hair.

I'm finally ready for you.
I untethered myself from those who can't love me.

I ripped my arms free from old promises.
I burned away the dead growth.

I'm alone in a green clearing
beneath breathing stars.

There is space in my poems for you,
but you're no longer here.

I want to scream fuck
until I'm hoarse.
I want to cry
until I'm dehydrated.

You killed yourself and took your voice away from this world.
I will never know the taste of your fingers.

No town on this earth is better off without you.
No airport, wooden picnic table or ice cream parlor
will know us as a couple.

Alone, I walk alongside an ancestral river in Missoula.
Her voice reaches out like a mother who wants to protect me.

She sings this in my ear:
You must let go of all that cannot be.
God will never take away everything that loves you.

Spring Thaw

I have no lover.
I have no beautiful man's voice
declaring his devotion to me.

My arms are not swimming
in an ocean of love songs.

All of this is true.
It seems like I should be sad.
Too often, loneliness
has been as familiar to me as yellow
cracked leaf autumn dissolving
into winter white and frost.

I'm alone.
Pieces of me are drifting and aligning in new ways.
The perfect stillness in my home feels electric.
Alone, I light white candles
and dance to the radio.
Alone, I am a spring thaw river
melting back into myself.

My Wild Horse of a Heart

My heart was born into this world
with the strength and beauty of a wild horse,
and she has needed every bit of that strength
to pull me through nights when I led us astray.
I have been lost in moonless lands
where my bearings swam away from me,
but in the stillness of canyon deep sorrow,
she heard me breathing.
In times of debilitating fear,
my wild horse of a heart could see
what I could not.
I trust her knowing eyes.
Her back is strong enough to carry me home
again and again.

Step Into the Light

Every good story that flies into my heart reminds me of what I really know.

I pray these stories are like a blue bird or a purple flower
or some other piece of beauty that flies in your path when you least expect it.
I pray each of these stories reminds you that your voice is meant to be loved.
Today, be a rainstorm of dances. Sing your way back to yourself.
Your spirit is here right now. There's always more to life than you know.
Every part of me that loves to laugh, sing and dance is here right now,
and I am strong because I accept my strength like the earth accepts rain.
Today the blessings run like rivers through all of us.

I'm sorry for all the times your heart's been broken,
but your heart still believes in love, even if you don't.
Your heart still needs love as much as it always has.
If I could hold each of you I would.
Sometimes, you must find a way to see your own goodness
because that's what holds you.

Your heart is braver than you know.
No matter what we have not done or did not say,
there is hope for us, all of us.
We must stop defining ourselves by who did not love us.
Do not let people who don't love you decide how much you're worth.
Do not let the people who think you're invisible
decide which parts of yourself you see.
Step into the light no matter how much darkness there's been.

You have always been worth fighting for.
You have always been worth standing up for.
You have always been worth dancing for.
You have always been worth singing for.
Today, start singing back your beauty.
Stand up for yourself.
Don't fight your doubts; just let them walk away.
Get up and dance for yourself.
Dance for all that is good. Dance for who you really are
because you're still here, and
I believe in all of you. I believe in all of us.

The real you is still here.
Your spirit has always been faithful to you.
Your spirit is still by your side waiting for you to ask it to dance.

44

Chapter 2 FAREWELL

Divorce Day

Today, I wore a purple sweater, went to court and got divorced.
Plates and saucers of snow covered the cold, soggy ground like old wedding dishes
thrown outside after a fight. I thought about buying myself something beautiful to
boost my spirits on such a day to mark the first and only divorce I've ever had.
I didn't buy myself anything because I didn't have the heart to be inside under
florescent lights. I walked alone down a cold street in black shoes, and I did not have
the energy to wish for anything except for a little rest from bottomless frigid anxiety.

I had a deep animal, mammal need to feel warm and protected.
I bought myself a hot coffee and a cup of soup, and I sat alone and swallowed heat.
Some days, I do not have the energy to cry.
I wish I felt more comfortable swearing in public.

This day, the day I used the legal system to break up with a man,
a young woman typed up the judge's words declaring me single.
I will have to wait for the official paperwork to arrive in the mail
to put my bank account in my own name, even though only my money is in it.

I am days past tired and sleep deprived. Tonight, a fat owl hurled itself against my car
as I drove down the highway. I'm not exactly sure what to think about the death of
married me and the resurrection of my maiden name.

I am afraid to live with a man again. Eventually, I will have another lover, and I am
certain I will not wash his socks or ever want to iron his shirts.
Doing for others what they would never do for me gets fucking old.
Oh, I am not above listening to sad songs and eating popcorn by myself out of self-pity.

I must accept that for the foreseeable future, my mood will not be boosted by anything.
I have to remind myself that sadness is forgivable, and even this sorrow will not be forever.

For So Long

Once, a young, beautiful man in a white t-shirt stood in a window.
I could see him from the wobbly and worn wooden table
in the hippie restaurant filled with people who didn't comb their hair.
I drank unsweetened coffee alone.

I thought of you.

For so long, all I could see was how handsome
you were in any kind of light.

These days, your hands look strange.
My love for your fingers on my skin is as far away
as any country I couldn't place on a map and will never visit.

I constantly ask myself how
could I so madly love every piece of a man
who did not see any beauty in my face?

Only now am I mature enough to realize
I will never fully understand my own heart.

I'm sure my heart had her reasons for loving you.
She and I both have our reasons for having to say so long.

Lost at Sea

It's been too long since I've seen the ocean.
It's January, and I know it's too cold to swim,
but I want the sound of waves to cover me while I sleep.
I want to stand close enough to the ocean to feel like I could be washed away.

The first time I saw the ocean, I was 19.
I stood at the edge of ice cold waves next to you.
I felt connected to foreign lands I couldn't see.
We walked along empty beaches in the wintertime,
our voices buried under slapping, whipping waves.
I couldn't hear you say my name.

Now, your voice is miles away because you live in a different home.
To my heart, you are lost at sea, never to return.

Sick

Last night, I could feel the undeniable signs.
My chest burned inside like a dull, scratched lantern.

My shoulders were tired.

As I talked to my ex-husband on the phone,
it felt like I inhaled fiber glass.

This is the first time I've been sick alone.

When I was married, my ex-husband
never brought me a drink of water or a cough drop.

It's not like I've ever been pampered or waited on.

Yet, it feels depressing to be sick and still have to cook dinner,
wash the dishes, and have no other adult in the house.

It hurts to swallow. It feels like I've been beaten with a rolling pin.

This, along with the dead mouse I had to get rid of a few days ago,
almost, *almost* makes me miss having a man in the house.

Sadness

Sometimes sadness threatens to pull me out to sea so far that I can't see the shore.
I feel surrounded by crashing waves on all sides, murkiness beneath my bare feet.
Sometimes, the beautiful sky feels too far away to hear me.
I feel alone with perfume on my neck and nobody to look me in the eye.

Sometimes, memories of moments long forgotten wash upon the shore
like shards of a broken rowboat, like the time you left me at a party without saying goodbye.
Sometimes, I find shrapnel of my girl self along dirt roads at the end of summer.

My throat bruises with sorrow like a smashed red apple.
Unspent grief crowds my pockets, heavy like hundreds of dollars in silver change
I can't carry.

How will I find the strength to swim against freezing, numbing currents of grief?
Will the tsunamis of rejection in my chest eventually erupt into a yellow morning
that smells like wind and the sounds of seagulls?

9

Gone

Kind words seemed to rip themselves out of your hands like kites on short strings
gone to the sky before I could touch them or hear them.

Words are my tattered paintbrushes, my calligraphy, my directions home.

I keep telling myself that deep down you wanted to give me words
that were beautiful and spiritual as the breath of a sleeping infant.

I must find a way to fit all these old longings into a green glass bottle
and throw them to the ocean.

Maybe some handsome man who doesn't speak English
will find my words washed upon a foreign shore and see beauty in the shapes of my letters.

How Are You?

What am I supposed to say when someone asks me how I am?
I'm always polite and say "Fine, how are you?" and keep on walking and smiling.

When, usually, what I feel like saying is this.
"What? How the fuck am I?
I am not okay.
I can barely speak because I am an ocean of sadness.
I am plagued with nightmares that have really strong hands.
I cried before breakfast, and I am almost too tired to comb my hair."

What else can I say? It's just easier to lie sometimes.

Position

Once, I was a young girl in uncomfortable shoes
with hair stiff as Styrofoam. At 18, I decided to walk away from all I knew
and look for myself in places I'd never been.

That was so long ago. I'm now nearly 40, and I keep shifting plates,
couches, and photographs around my house.
I sweep floors, chop wood, mow the lawn, stand at a stove and cook food.

I keep rubbing my shoulder and stretching my ankles.
I'm trying to find a more comfortable way to be in this position.

Calgary

Once, the skin on my eyelids was inflamed
pink and bleeding. It hurt to blink.
Our daughter was three. Our son was less than a year old.
We drove to Canada to take them to the zoo.
I was so uncomfortable with your anger
as we drove into a foreign country with two little kids.

Your moods reminded me of snow in August or hail storms
with fist sized balls of ice beating dents into cars.
Whenever I felt like a cloudless sky or calm water,
one of your dark moods could blow frigid winds
between the words of our conversations.

The radio played songs I remembered from high school.
As we drove through miles of Canadian prairie,
I kept thinking about how I hadn't always felt so sad
and too tired to care much about the beauty
of nighttime skies pregnant with moonlight.

For some unknown reason, you weren't speaking to me,
and I was trying to pretend everything was okay
because it was our vacation, and I was paying for it.
My eyelids were cracked and bleeding because stress
always takes a toll on my skin. Whether it's tears or blood,
sorrow always find a way to break through the surface of me.

What Wasn't Said

Thanks for teaching our kids how to identify various hawks.
Thanks for teaching them how to identify animals by their poop.
Thanks for teaching them how to shoot guns and catch fish.

Because of you, our kids know how to use a pigeon as bait to catch another bird.
Because of you, our kids have handled decaying turtle shells.
Because of you, I found bird feet and dead chicks in pants pockets at laundry time.
Because of you, I once owned a rooster flock and two bad goats.
Because of you, I was married for 15 years.
Because of you, I have three kids I will love forever.

Not Everything

With short skirts, bare legs, and my hair in a ponytail,
and my face unlined, you once kissed poetry into my hands.
We lived in a yellow house where I lit blue candles.

Years later, army men lived under our couch, and there were papers everywhere:
old spelling tests and crooked sentences scrawled by rough little hands.

Now, I am your former wife, and our oldest child is nearly a teenager.
Things evolved in ways I never could have predicted,
but not everything was a waste of my time.

I'm Grateful

or the times I had your black shirts folded in my hands.
I stacked them for you to slide against your bare back
after you showered and washed your hair.

For years, I washed plates after you ate mashed potatoes or spaghetti off them.

Countless times, I lay awake in bed waiting for the sound of your car to stop in the driveway,
and the slam of the car door, and your hand on the door knob to our house.
I'd wake from the warmest sleep to hear about your night.

I convinced myself your voice was all I needed,
your words against my face would hold me like a picture on a wall.

I thought walking alone with the smell of you in my hair would be enough.
I was wrong about so many things.
I thought I would always want you to put my face in your hands and hum a song in my ear.

I used to wish you would never stop coming home to me.
I thought you would always shine in some part of me.

The way I used to want you is a galaxy I left behind and flew away from.
I cannot go back in time. The universe would not allow it, even *if* I wanted to see you again.

Joined

At our wedding, someone gave us white ceramic birds, and someone else gave
us a cookbook with a recipe from Portales, New Mexico where I met you.

Once, we woke at the crack of dawn to catch a boat from Martha's Vineyard to Nantucket.
I saw a famous guy walking down the street.
On the boat, I stood alone on the deck, and drops of ocean splashed my face,
and I loved the smell of the salty water on me and on you.

Years later, when a baby died inside my body, you held my hand because I needed your hand.
I was afraid I would never be able to stop crying.

One year, I forgot our anniversary, and I wept when you sent me flowers,
so moved that even though you hadn't seen my face in months, you thought of me.

From the day I met you, I loved your hands, and how they were always warmer than mine.
You often rubbed your hands together and put my fingers between your palms to warm them.

For many reasons, I had to leave you and your name, and your hands behind.
I will never let you hold me or my fingers ever again.

I used to pray that God would show me the way to a sliver of hope.

Do you know I still pray for you?
I pray I can forgive you, even though you never apologized for anything.
I pray you can forgive yourself for letting me go.

Blessing

Once, my tooth cracked open, and each time I breathed,
pain pulsated, blossomed like spilled ink in my mouth.

I was broke and couldn't afford to see the dentist,
and had nothing valuable enough to sell.

You gave me money to see a dentist.
I was so grateful.
I loved you so much.

The dentist turned out to be unlicensed.
Because of his work, I wound up with an infection and a fake tooth.

That was many years ago
when you still wanted to wake up with me every morning.
I didn't have lines in my forehead,
and I was nobody's mother.

You'll no longer swim with me at night, and you won't
kiss any songs into my hair, and you can't help me
when my chest feels like a broken ceramic plate.
But once, you were a blessing to me like the smell of lilac
blowing through an open window after a long winter.

All I Can Give You is This

If I could, I would put a purple lilac in your hand
so you could put the smell of something tender from me against your face one more time.
I would give you something beautiful that's already dead.

You gave me your youth as faithfully as May flowers leap from the earth to the sun,
and I loved every single petal of you.
Each night beneath the stars with you used to feel like a gift.

I used to want you to embrace me one more time and kiss my hair like moonlight,
and now I don't. I'm sorry for each terrible second of everything that happened to you
that made you feel so unworthy of me long before my hands touched your face.

Concert

You couldn't identify one song by the Black Crowes but agreed to go to the concert
with me. They were my favorite band in high school and college.
Listening to their songs reminds me of when your mouth tasted like music.

Rain soaked us down to the underwear. After it snowed sideways, they canceled
the show. On the bus back to Missoula, there was no place to sit, so we stood
in the aisles while guys smoked marijuana that smelled like burning rubber and melting plastic.

It was unlike you not to complain, but you didn't say a word. That concert was years ago.

Now, we are no longer a couple. My hands no longer want you.
I can't remember what you taste like, but I remember moments when being with you felt good.

Saving Myself

For years, I submerged myself
beneath your junk mail clutter & angry words.
I held my breath waiting
for the surface of my life to get smoother.

My lungs were going to implode
& I had to decide to stay where I was
or swim to a choppy surface.

So, I let your hand go
& I floated right to the top
of a huge mess.
I'm sorry I left you there,
but drowning people
usually kill those who try to save them.

I'm Here

The smell of heavy wet snow and wood sap smells like home to me.
I love this place, but I still miss New Mexico sometimes.
I used to wear small dresses and leave lipstick marks on my lover's beard.
I loved him in the darkness of early morning.
I floated in the smell of his shirts.

Once in a while, my empty hands reach for his back that's an island far away from me.
Sometimes, I have anchor heavy sadness in my throat,
and I have to remind myself of where I am right now.
I must wade through knee deep snow and sort through old feelings.
I must find a way to get my bearings straight,
so I can someday be brave enough to enter love's waters again.

Dear College That Sent Me Two Rejection Letters,

How have you been without me? Years ago, I applied for a job there. I was 25, fresh out of grad school. Okay, I admit, I didn't really want to live in Alaska. I was afraid to live in a house made of scraps. I was afraid of what 24 hours of darkness would do to me. I was afraid I would get depressed, start smoking pot or get mauled by a caribou. But the thought of being broke *and* educated was even worse, so I applied for a job in Alaska.

I didn't hear from you, so I moved to Montana. I found a job working in a gift shop selling t-shirts. I was insanely in debt with student loans, so I sold silver rings and bags of polished rocks. Finally, one day, I got a letter from you. I tore it open. Rejection! I cried with disappointment before I went back to the gift shop.

Eventually, the summer ended. I got a job with a retirement plan and paid time off. Months passed. I was so over you. Then, when I least expected it, I got a letter from you out of the blue. My chest tightened. You changed your mind? You wanted me? Thoughts of moving flashed through my mind. I ripped open the letter. WTF! A second rejection letter. I laughed and cried at the same time.

Why had I given you this power over me? I felt like a mail order bride rejected by the same creepy guy I didn't really want... twice. Once, I was ready to move and change my whole life for you. I would have given you the best years of my life, my childbearing years. Bastard. I'm glad you rejected me. If you ever send me another letter, I will not open it.

Sincerely,
Jennifer

Away From You

There is an orange butterfly buried inside your chest,
and it will never get out again.

Perhaps it flew inside you when you screamed your first sounds into the world.
Perhaps God breathed it into you before you were a lump of flesh.

Your love for me has tired wings.
In a few moments of unguardedness, your love for me fluttered weakly in sunlight.

Your chest is a dark cage filled with mystery and blinded beauty.
After all these years of offering my hand to you,
I am tired of you biting me with ugly words.

I am so tired that all I want to do is find a soft piece of grass and press my back against it.
All I want to do is get rained on beneath the sky.
I want to sink and rise in any ocean and swim far away from you.

I am no longer sorry for giving up on whatever little piece of good is left in your heart.
I'm sure there is something beautiful left inside you, but I will no longer seek it.

Whatever flicker of love or kindness is left inside you rests between you and God.
Today, I will put my hand on my own bare neck and tell myself that I'll be okay
without your love because I never really held it.

Today, I will swim cold in autumn waters. I will let sunlight take me in.
I will let the sound of wind blowing through orange leaves serenade me.
Faithful white birds and black birds will fly circles across my path
singing out to my face to tell me that I am not alone or unloved.

Farewell

I could paint every wall in my house with red words
I would like to say to you, but you would not read any of them.

I could carve one poem into my right arm with a broken toothpick,
and it would not hurt as much as having to walk away from you.

Made in United States
Troutdale, OR
10/12/2023

13641449R00042